PowerKids Readers:

The Bilingual Library of the United States of America™

OREGON
OREGÓN

JENNIFER WAY

TRADUCCIÓN AL ESPAÑOL: MARÍA CRISTINA BRUSCA

The Rosen Publishing Group's
PowerKids Press™ & **Editorial Buenas Letras**™
New York

Published in 2006 by The Rosen Publishing Group, Inc.
29 East 21st Street, New York, NY 10010

First Edition

Book Design: Albert B. Hanner
Photo Credits: Cover, p. 30 (state motto) © Connie Ricca/Corbis; p. 5 © Joseph Sohm; ChromoSohhm Inc./Corbis; p. 7, 31 (border) © Geoatlas; p. 9, 30 (state nickname), 31 (volcano) © Craig Tuttle/Corbis; p. 11 © James Leynse/Corbis; p. 13, 30 (state flower) Albert B. Hanner; p. 15, 31 (pioneers), (Ginger Rogers) © Bettmann/Corbis; p. 17, 31 (Beverly Cleary) © Harper Collins; p. 19 © Greg Ebersole/Associated Press, Longview Daily News; p. 21 © Buddy Mays/Corbis; p. 23 © Don Ryan/Associated Press, AP; p. 25, 30 (capital) © Doug Wilson/Corbis; p. 30 (bird) © Michael Gore; Frank Lane Picture Agency/Corbis, (state tree) © Paul A. Souders/Corbis, (Herbert Hoover) © Corbis; p. 31 (Chief Joseph) © Christie's Images/Corbis, 31 (Danny Glover) © Eddie Adams/Corbis, (Matt Groening) © MC Leod Murdo/Corbis SYGMA, 31 (fur) © Lowell Georgia/Corbis.

Library of Congress Cataloging-in-Publication Data

Way, Jennifer.
Oregon / Jennifer Way ; traducción al español, María Cristina Brusca. — 1st ed.
p. cm. — (The bilingual library of the United States of America)
Includes bibliographical references and index.
ISBN 1-4042-3102-1 (lib. binding)
1. Oregon—Juvenile literature. I. Title. II. Series.
F876.3.W39 2006
979.5—dc22
                                        2005020537

Manufactured in the United States of America

Due to the changing nature of Internet links, Editorial Buenas Letras has developed an online list of Web sites related to the subject of this book. This site is updated regularly. Please use this link to access the list:

http://www.buenasletraslinks.com/ls/oregon

Contents

Contenido

Welcome to Oregon

Oregon is the ninth largest state in the United States. Oregon is known as the Beaver State. The beaver is Oregon's state animal.

Bienvenidos a Oregón

Por su tamaño, Oregón es el noveno estado de los Estados Unidos. Oregón es conocido como el Estado Castor. El castor es el animal oficial del estado de Oregón.

Oregon Flag and State Seal

Bandera y escudo de Oregón

Oregon Geography

Oregon is in the Pacific Northwest of the United States. Oregon borders California, Idaho, Nevada and Washington. The Pacific Ocean is on the western coast of Oregon.

Geografía de Oregón

Oregón está en el noroeste de los Estados Unidos. Oregón linda con los estados de California, Idaho, Nevada y Washington. La frontera occidental del estado es el océano Pacífico.

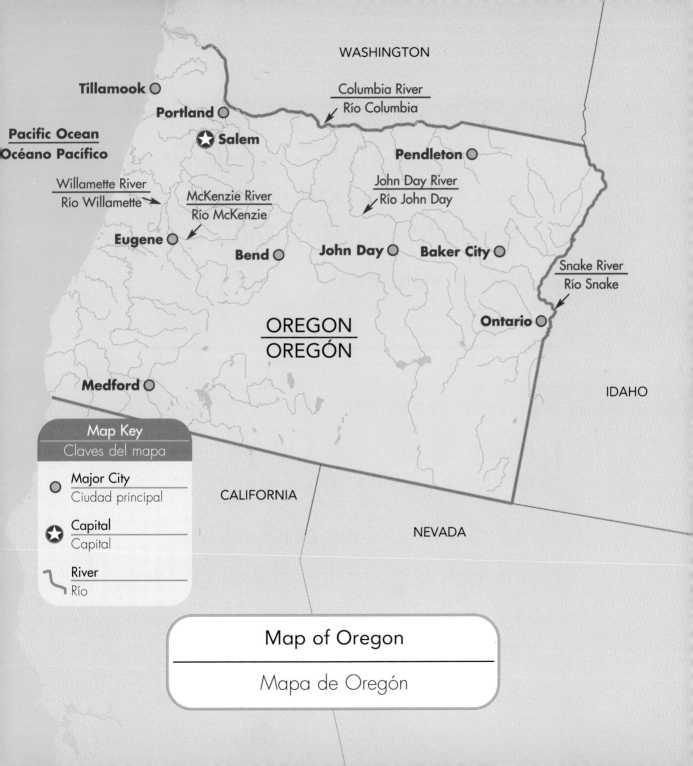

WASHINGTON

Tillamook ○

Pacific Ocean
Océano Pacífico

Portland ○

★ Salem

Columbia River
Río Columbia

Pendleton ○

Willamette River
Río Willamette →

McKenzie River
Río McKenzie

John Day River
Río John Day

Eugene ○

Bend ○

John Day ○

Baker City ○

Snake River
Río Snake

OREGON
OREGÓN

Ontario ○

IDAHO

Medford ○

Map Key
Claves del mapa

○ Major City
Ciudad principal

★ Capital
Capital

River
Río

CALIFORNIA

NEVADA

Map of Oregon

Mapa de Oregón

Mount Hood is Oregon's highest point at 11,239 feet (3,426 m). Mount Hood is part of the Cascade Mountains. Mount Hood is also a volcano.

La cumbre del monte Hood es el punto más alto de Oregón. Tiene 11,239 pies (3,426 m) de altura. El monte Hood es parte de las montañas Cascade. El monte Hood es también un volcán.

Mount Hood and Beaver Pond

El monte Hood y la laguna Beaver

Oregon History

Sacagawea was a Shoshone Native American woman. She guided the explorers Lewis and Clark during their travels in the western United States. She brought them to Oregon in 1805.

Historia de Oregón

Sacagawea fue una mujer nativo americana de la tribu Shoshone. Sacagawea guió a los exploradores Meriwether Lewis y William Clark en su viaje hacia el oeste de los Estados Unidos. En 1805, Sacagawea los llevó a Oregón.

Dollar Coins Honoring Sacagawea

Monedas de un dólar en honor a Sacagawea

John McLoughlin is known as the Father of Oregon. He came to Oregon in 1824 as a fur trader. McLoughlin helped other settlers to withstand the hard conditions of the land.

John McLoughlin es conocido como el Padre de Oregón. Llegó a Oregón en 1824 como comerciante de pieles. McLoughlin ayudó a otros colonos a resistir las duras condiciones de la región.

John McLoughlin (1784–1857)

In the 1840s many people began to move west to places like Oregon. They were called pioneers. The pioneers traveled in wagons on the Oregon Trail. The Oregon Trail is a road from Missouri to Oregon.

En la década de 1840, mucha gente comenzó a emigrar al oeste. Estas personas se llamaron pioneros. Viajaron en carretas por la Ruta de Oregón. Esta ruta es un camino entre Misuri y Oregón.

A Family of Pioneers with a Covered Wagon

Una familia de pioneros y su carreta

Beverly Cleary is a children's book writer. Her Ramona books are loved by readers and have won many prizes. She was born in 1916 in McMinville, Oregon, and grew up in Yamhill and Portland.

Beverly Cleary es una escritora de libros para niños. Su serie sobre la pequeña Ramona es muy apreciada y ha ganado muchos premios. Cleary nació en 1916, en McMinville, Oregón y creció en Yamhill y Portland.

Beverly Cleary

Living in Oregon

People from all over the world have made Oregon their home. Oregonians have events to honor all the different countries from which they have come.

La vida en Oregón

En Oregón vive gente de todo el mundo. La gente de Oregón celebra eventos en honor a los países de donde proviene.

Cinco de Mayo Celebration in Salem, Oregon

Celebración del Cinco de Mayo en Salem, Oregón

Oregon is known for its forests, beaches and farms. The Deschutes National Forest and the Willamette National Forest are two of Oregon's largest forests.

Oregón es conocido por sus bosques, playas y granjas.
El Bosque Nacional Deschutes y el Bosque Nacional Willamette son dos de los más grandes de Oregón.

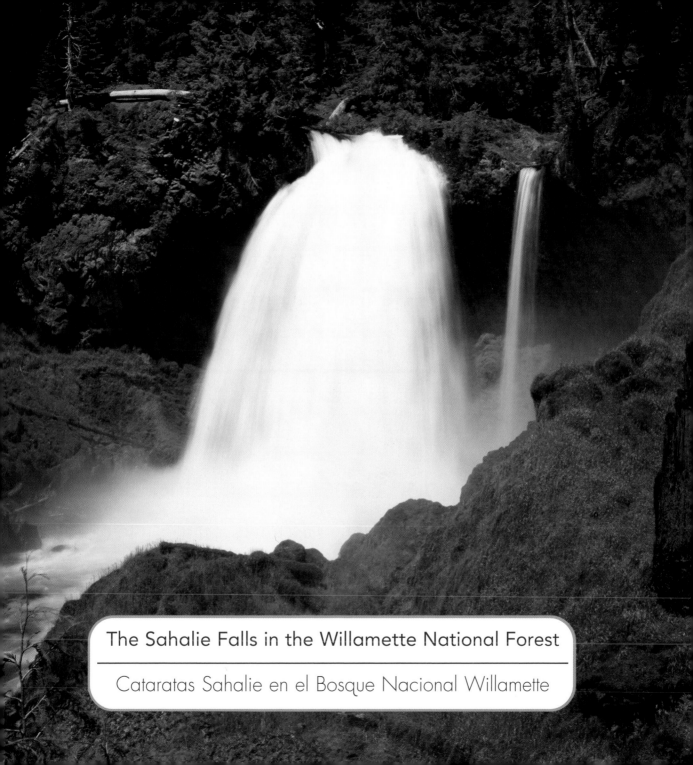

The Sahalie Falls in the Willamette National Forest

Cataratas Sahalie en el Bosque Nacional Willamette

Oregon Today

At the Oregon Museum of Science and Industry in Portland you can learn about dinosaurs and many other things. It is one of the most visited science museums in the country.

Oregón, hoy

En el Museo de Ciencia e Industria de Oregón, en Portland, puedes aprender sobre los dinosaurios y muchas otras cosas. Es uno de los museos de ciencia más visitados del país.

Oregon Museum of Science and Industry

Museo de Ciencia e Industria de Oregón

Portland, Eugene, and Salem are the biggest cities in Oregon. Salem is the capital of the state of Oregon.

Portland, Eugene y Salem son las ciudades más grandes de Oregón. Salem es la capital del estado de Oregón.

State Capitol Building in Salem, Oregon

Capitolio del estado en Salem, Oregón

Activity:
Let's Draw the Map of Oregon

Actividad:
Dibujemos el mapa de Oregón

1

Begin your map of Oregon with a rectangular guide.

Comienza tu mapa de Oregón trazando un rectángulo como guía.

2

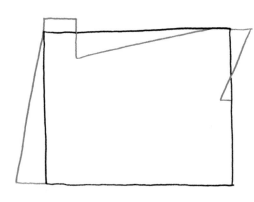

Draw a rough outline for Oregon's borders, using the rectangle as a guide, as shown.

Traza el contorno de Oregón, imitando el ejemplo que ves aquí.

26

3

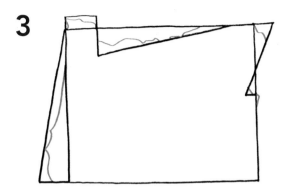

Next draw the Pacific coast and Oregon's border with Washington using squiggly lines. Draw Oregon's eastern border using a squiggly line and a straight line.

Ahora, dibuja la costa del Pacífico y la frontera entre Washington y Oregón trazando líneas cortas y curvas. Dibuja la frontera oriental de Oregón trazando una línea recta y varias líneas cortas y curvas.

4

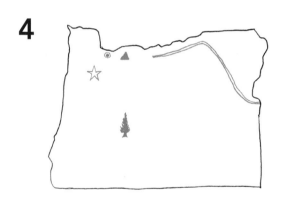

Add a star for Salem. Draw two lines for the Oregon Trail. Add a dot with a circle for the city of Portland. Add a triangle for Mount Hood. Add a tree for the Deschutes National Forest.

Agrega una estrella en el lugar de la capital, Salem. Dibuja la Ruta de Oregón con dos líneas. Añade un punto con un círculo en el sitio de la ciudad de Portland. Añade un triángulo que represente al monte Hood. Agrega un árbol en el lugar del Bosque Nacional Deschutes.

Timeline		Cronología
Spanish explorers see the Oregon coast for the first time.	**1543**	Exploradores españoles descubren la costa de Oregón.
The fur trade begins along the Pacific coast.	**1778**	Comienza el comercio de pieles a lo largo de la costa del Pacífico.
Lewis and Clark reach Oregon on their Voyage of Discovery.	**1805**	Lewis y Clark llegan a Oregón en su viaje de descubrimiento.
The Oregon Trail brings white settlers to Oregon.	**1840**	La ruta de Oregón atrae a colonos blancos a Oregón.
Salem is named Oregon's capital.	**1852**	Salem es nombrada capital de Oregón.
Oregon becomes a state on February 14.	**1859**	El 14 de febrero, Oregón se convierte en estado.
The volcano Mount St. Helens blows up.	**1980**	Hace erupción el volcán Mount St. Helens.
Barbara Roberts becomes Oregon's first woman governor.	**1991**	Barbara Roberts es la primera mujer en ocupar el cargo de gobernadora de Oregón.

Oregon Events

January
Robert Burns Dinner (Scottish celebration), Welches

February
Chinese New Year Parade and Celebration, Jacksonville
Frontier Heritage Fair, Eugene

May
Cinco de Mayo Fiesta, Portland

June
Sandcastle Contest, Cannon Beach

July
Cherry Days, Hood River
Salem Art Festival

August
Hood to Coast Relay, Mt Hood to Seaside

October
Fall Kite Festival, Lincoln City

December
Snowflake Festival, Klamath Falls

Eventos en Oregón

Enero
Cena Robert Burns (celebración escocesa), en Welches

Febrero
Desfile y celebraciones del año nuevo chino, en Jacksonville
Feria de tradición de la frontera, en Eugene

Mayo
Fiesta del Cinco de Mayo, en Portland

Junio
Concurso de castillos de arena en Cannon Beach

Julio
Días de la cereza, en Hood River
Festival de arte de Salem

Agosto
Carrera de relevos de Hood a la costa, de Monte Hood a Seaside

Octubre
Festival de papalote de otoño en Lincoln City

Diciembre
Festival del copo de nieve, en Klamath Falls

Oregon Facts/Datos sobre Oregón

<u>Population</u> 3.5 million		<u>Población</u> 3.5 millones
<u>Capital</u> Salem		<u>Capital</u> Salem
<u>State Motto</u> *Alis Volat Propiis*, She Flies with Her Own Wings		<u>Lema del estado</u> *Alis Volat Propiis*, Ella vuela con alas propias
<u>State Flower</u> Oregon Grape		<u>Flor del estado</u> Uva de Oregón
<u>State Bird</u> Western Meadowlark		<u>Ave del estado</u> Pradero occidental
<u>State Nickname</u> The Beaver State		<u>Mote del estado</u> Estado Castor
<u>State Tree</u> Douglas Fir		<u>Árbol del estado</u> Abeto Douglas
<u>State Song</u> "Oregon, My Oregon"		<u>Canción del estado</u> "Oregón, mi Oregón"

Famous Oregonians/Oregoneses famosos

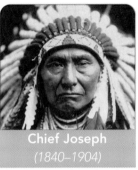

Chief Joseph
(1840–1904)

Native American leader
Líder nativo americano

Herbert Hoover
(1874–1964)

U.S. president
Presidente de E.U.A.

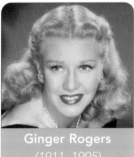

Ginger Rogers
(1911–1995)

Actress
Actriz

Beverly Cleary
(1916–   )

Children's book writer
Escritora de libros para niños

Danny Glover
(1947–   )

Actor
Actor

Matt Groening
(1954–   )

Creator of The Simpsons
Creador de Los Simpsons

Words to Know/Palabras que debes saber

OREGON

CALIFORNIA

border
frontera

fur
piel

pioneers
pioneros

volcano
volcán

Here are more books to read about Oregon:
Otros libros que puedes leer sobre Oregón:

In English/En inglés:

Oregon
by Ingram, Scott
Children's Press, 2000

Oregon
by Brindell Fradin, Dennis
Children's Press 1995

Words in English: 303

Palabras en español: 239

Index

Índice